Prince John
and the Unicorn

by

Don McCain

Illustrated by Brenda Ragsdale

Copyright © 2018; 2020 by Don McCain

Illustrated by Brenda Ragsdale

All rights reserved. No part of this publication may be reproduced, distributed, or transmitted in any form or by any means, including photocopying, recording, or other electronic or mechanical methods, without the prior written permission of the publisher, except in the case of brief quotations embodied in critical reviews and certain other noncommercial uses permitted by copyright law.

ISBN: 978-1-951300-84-5

Liberation's Publishing LLC
West Point, Mississippi
www.liberationspublishing.com

Prince John
and the Unicorn

by

Don McCain

Illustrated by Brenda Ragsdale

During a time that existed long ago, there lived a mystical wizard named Abdul in the Kingdom of Annandale. Abdul sought only power and glory, and in the village of Kearny, he was the most glorious and powerful. Kearny was in the East of Annandale and had the most majestic horses every bred. People from all over the world came to Kearny to buy, trade, and sell horses. There were horses of all sizes and color; they were fast and beautiful.

Abdul owned thirteen horses. His strongest horse was six feet at the shoulders and black as night. His fastest horse was pure white as snow and faster than any horse in the entire kingdom.

Abdul's house was large and roomy. It sat on acres of land surrounded by standing woods on the outskirts, with plenty of barns, sheds, and pastures for all his horses. He even had his own stream that bubbled with fresh water.

One day a handsome couple visited Abdul. It was Prince John and his beautiful young bride Olivia. They wanted to

buy two horses. The couple talked to Abdul about their intentions to buy horses and all the while, Abdul became smitten by Oliva's beauty.

The couple made their choice; it was Abdul's finest horses, Big Fellow the strong black one and Full Cloud the fast white one. Not knowing Abdul was an evil wizard, they continued to bargain.

"I'll trade you these horses for this beautiful lady," Abdul said to Prince John.

Prince John became angry right away. "She is my new bride," he said forcefully. "A million majestic horses could not equal her value to me!"

Prince John took his bride by the hand and walked away hurriedly. Abdul ran along side them, stepped in front of them, and blew magical powder into Prince John's face. Prince John felt weak; his knees buckled, and he fell to the ground. Immediately after, Prince John turned into a

brilliant blue unicorn.

Prince John the Unicorn stood up on his feet, threw his mane into the air, and reared up on his hind feet. He kicked out his back hooves and came down on all four, placing them firmly on the ground. He then nudged Abdul forcefully in the chest with his nose. Olivia fainted, and Abdul laughed a wicked laugh.

When Olivia awoke, she found herself stretched out on a bed before an open window. Outside she could see Prince John the Unicorn, beautiful and brilliant in a fenced in area. Abdul came into the room with a tray of food and a glass of wine. He walked to the edge of her bed. Towering over her, he looked down and said,

"You are mine now, my lovely. You will do as I say, or you will never see Prince John in his human form again."

Olivia sobbed and looked out of the window towards Prince John the Unicorn. He was watching Olivia the entire time. He stood there pawing the ground with his front right hoof, with his ears pinned back to his head.

"I will be right back my pretty," laughed Abdul. Olivia covered her head with a pillow and cried.

After thirty-minutes had passed, there was a knock at the door. Olivia did not respond; She was sure Abdul had returned. To her surprise, a humble looking old lady walked in. She wore a cotton gray colored dress with a white apron tied around the waist. She hurried to Olivia's side. "Don't be afraid my child," she said to her, "I am here to help you escape." Olivia was happy, but nervous. "Abdul is my son," the nice lady continued. "He is my son and an evil man."

Olivia shook with fear. She was nervous and cold. Abdul's mother closed the window and took out of her pocket a purple bag with a drawstring. "Take this," she said moving quickly. "Flee! Get on your blue unicorn and race away from here like the wind. Once you are beyond the pastures and woods sprinkle the powder inside this purple bag into the unicorn's face."

"But," started Olivia.

"No buts! Just do it," Abdul's mother insisted.

Olivia jumped out of bed with no thoughts for shoes. She slid down the lattice that was up against her window. Once below she ran across the lawn, jumped the fence onto the back of Prince John the Unicorn. "Let's go John." She shouted.

Prince John the Unicorn ran in circles to build up enough speed and jumped the fence with ease.

He ran and ran beyond the pastures and woods just as Olivia instructed him. They stopped at a beautiful lake. Olivia gracefully slid from the back of Prince John the Unicorn. She stepped up to his head and hugged his face. Olivia opened the purple bag and pulled the drawstring. She grabbed a pinch of the powder blue dust placed it in her palm and blew it into Prince John the Unicorn's face.

Prince John the Unicorn turned into his old self. He and Olivia kissed and hugged then turned to walk the rest of the way to Annandale.

Time passed, and Prince John became king, and Olivia was a wise and beautiful queen. Both decided to take a visit to Abdul. The two of them along with the palace guards traveled to Kearny.

Abdul came out to meet them, obstinate as ever. He would not bow to the new king and queen. Olivia pulled the purple bag of magic dust from her purse. She reached into the bag with her index finger and thumb, took a pinch

of dust and placed it into the palm of her hand. She blew it into Abdul's face.

Abdul grew unsteady of his feet. He fainted and fell to the ground. When he got up, he was a donkey. His mother threw her hands up in exhilaration and kicked him. "For years," she said, "I have been your slave!"

"Not anymore!" declared King John. "From now on you will eat at our table. We will treat you as our mother."

"Bless you," she replied. "My name is Tesserae."

King John ordered the guard to help her pack all her belongings onto the back of Abdul the Donkey. Once at the kingdom, Abdul the Donkey pulled carts filled with manure from the king's stables for the rest of his life.

Queen Olivia of Annandale was the only one in the entire world who had the magic powder that turned ordinary horses into unicorns. That was the original purpose of the dust. She seldom used it, but one day she felt pity on Abdul the Donkey and turned him into a goat.

King John, Queen Olivia, and Tesserae lived happily ever after!

www.ingramcontent.com/pod-product-compliance
Lightning Source LLC
Chambersburg PA
CBHW042356280426
43661CB00095B/1134